CW01163731

TO DAVID, ALICE, ISABELLE, CAROLINE, IVY & IRIS;
WHO INSPIRED ME TO WRITE
ALL OF THIS NONSENSE.

Copyright © 2025 by Danielle K. Herker
All rights reserved. Published by Danielle K. Herker -Indy Pub, Whiddley Whompers, an imprint of Danielle K. Herker.
No part of this book may be reproduced or transmitted in any form, or by any means, electronic or mechanical, including photocopying, recording, or by any information storage and retrieval system, without written permission from the publisher.

First edition, January 2025

Names: Herker, Danielle K., author, illustrator
Title: The Night Defenders.
Summary: Bats are finally ready to tell the world about their heroic nighttime duties and reveal how other animals are unsuitable for this incredibly important job.
Identifiers: ISBN 9798348431976 (hardcover)
Subjects: Bedtime & Dreams- Juvenile Fiction, Animals/ Nocturnal- Juvenile Fiction,
Humorous Stories-Juvenile Fiction.

The Night Defenders

Written & Illustrated by Danielle K. Herker

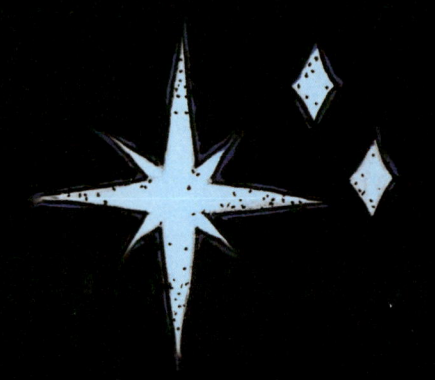

Did you know that bats watch over the night?

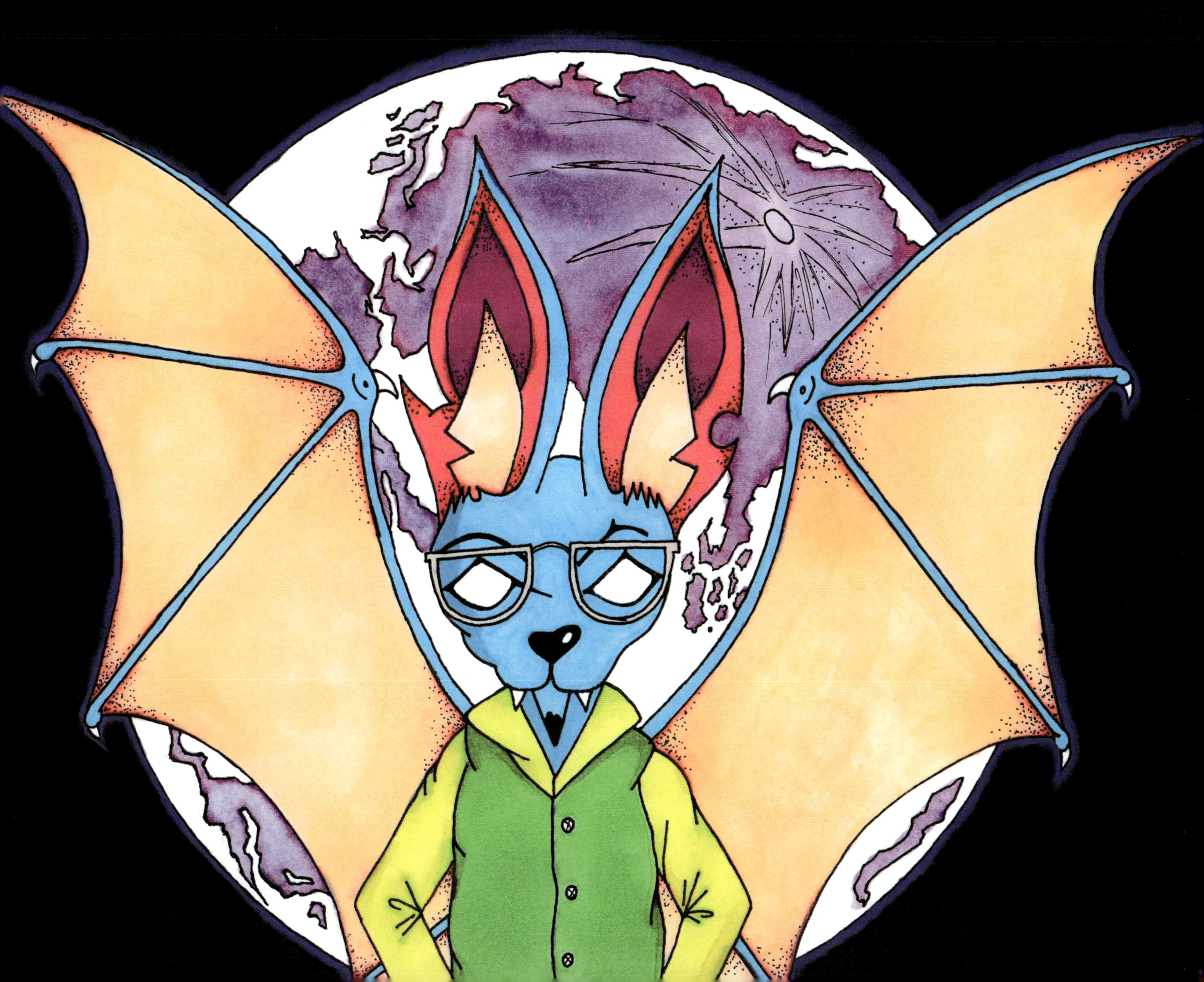

There are stories about owls watching over the night, but that is **NONSENSE!**

How can owls watch over the night when they can't keep their heads straight?

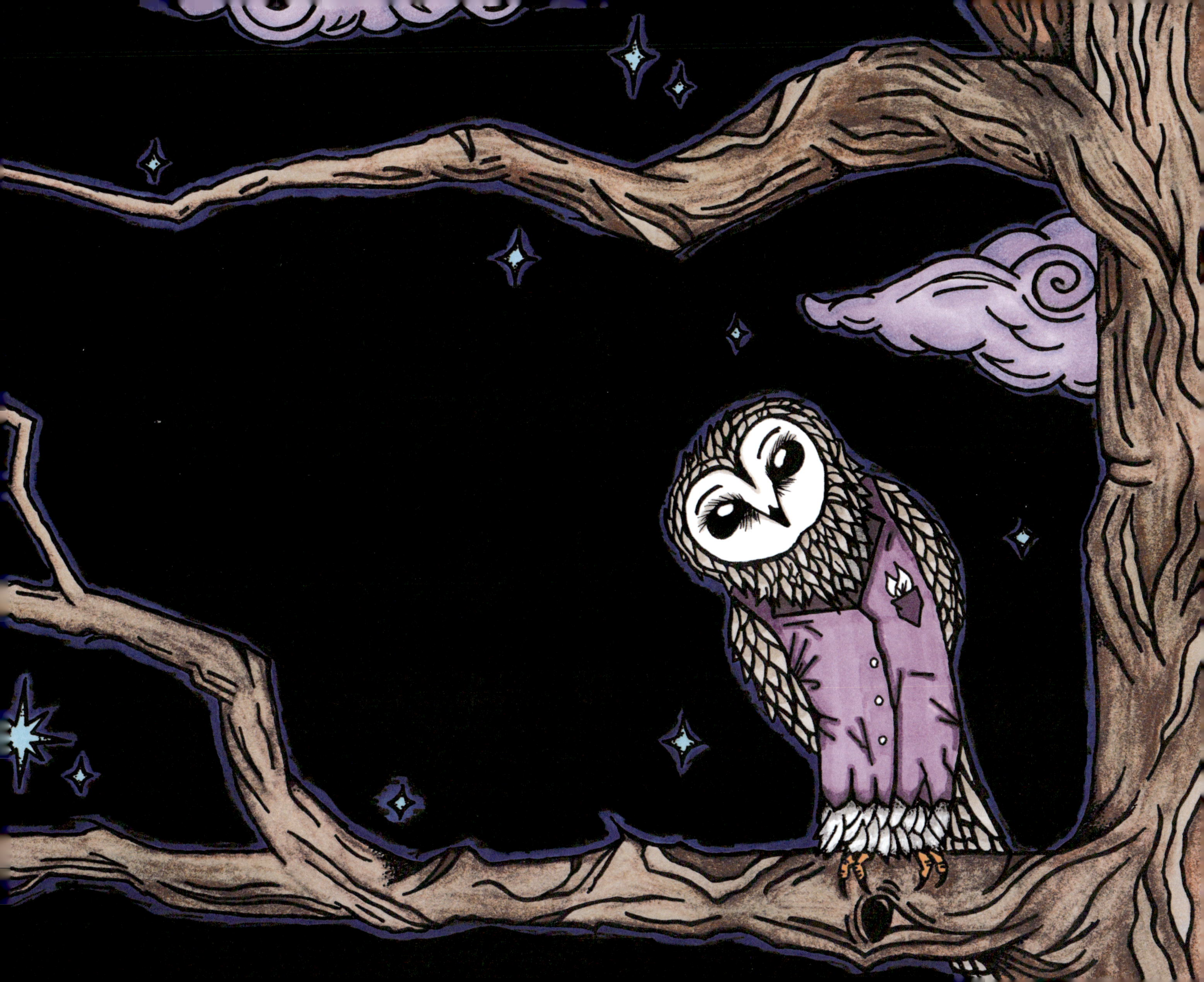

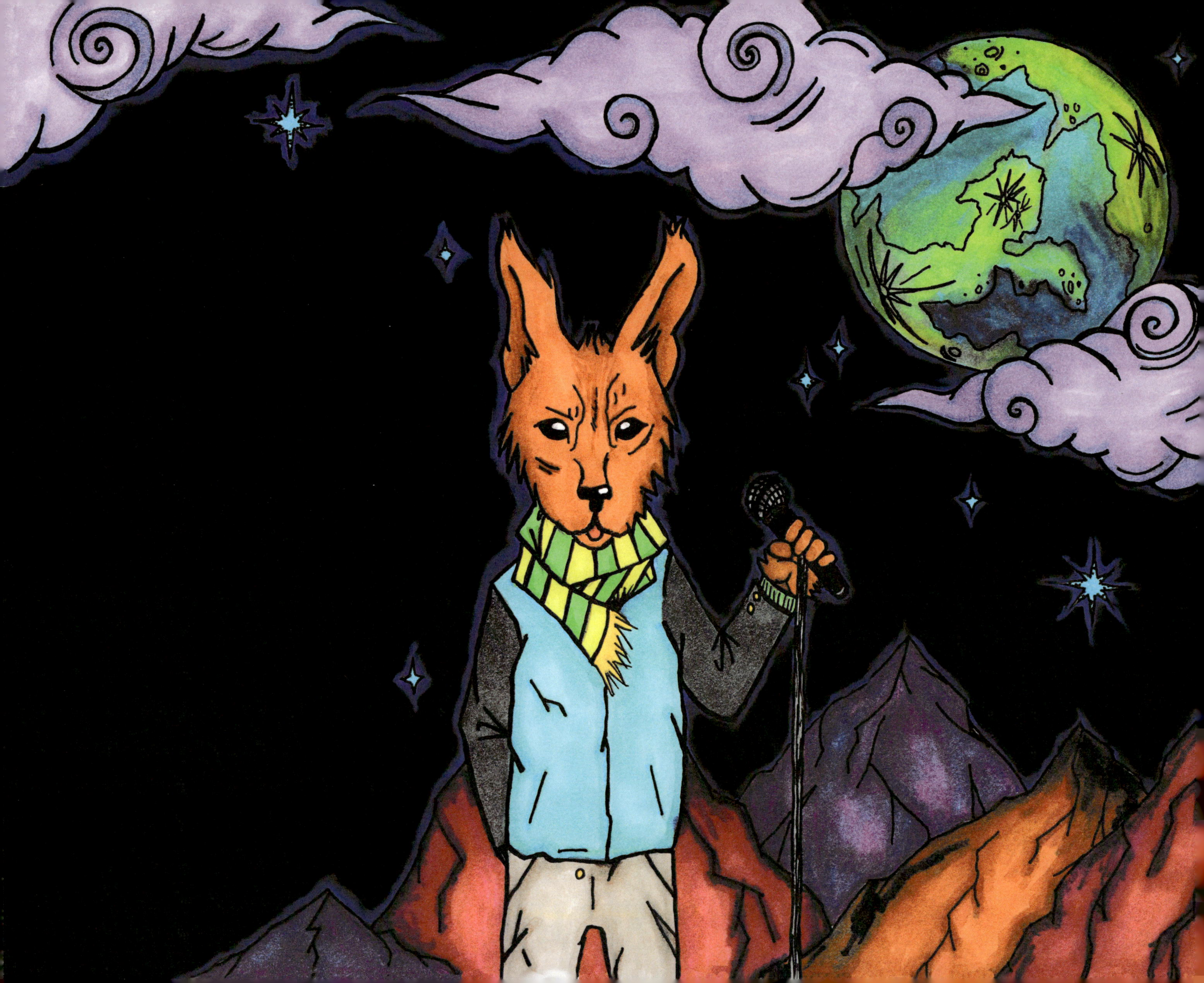

Other people think that wolves are in charge of the night.

How can wolves do the job? Especially when they are too busy singing to the moon!

Some kids might ask, "What about raccoons?" Are you serious?

How can the raccoons watch over the night when they spend all of their time searching for buried treasure?!

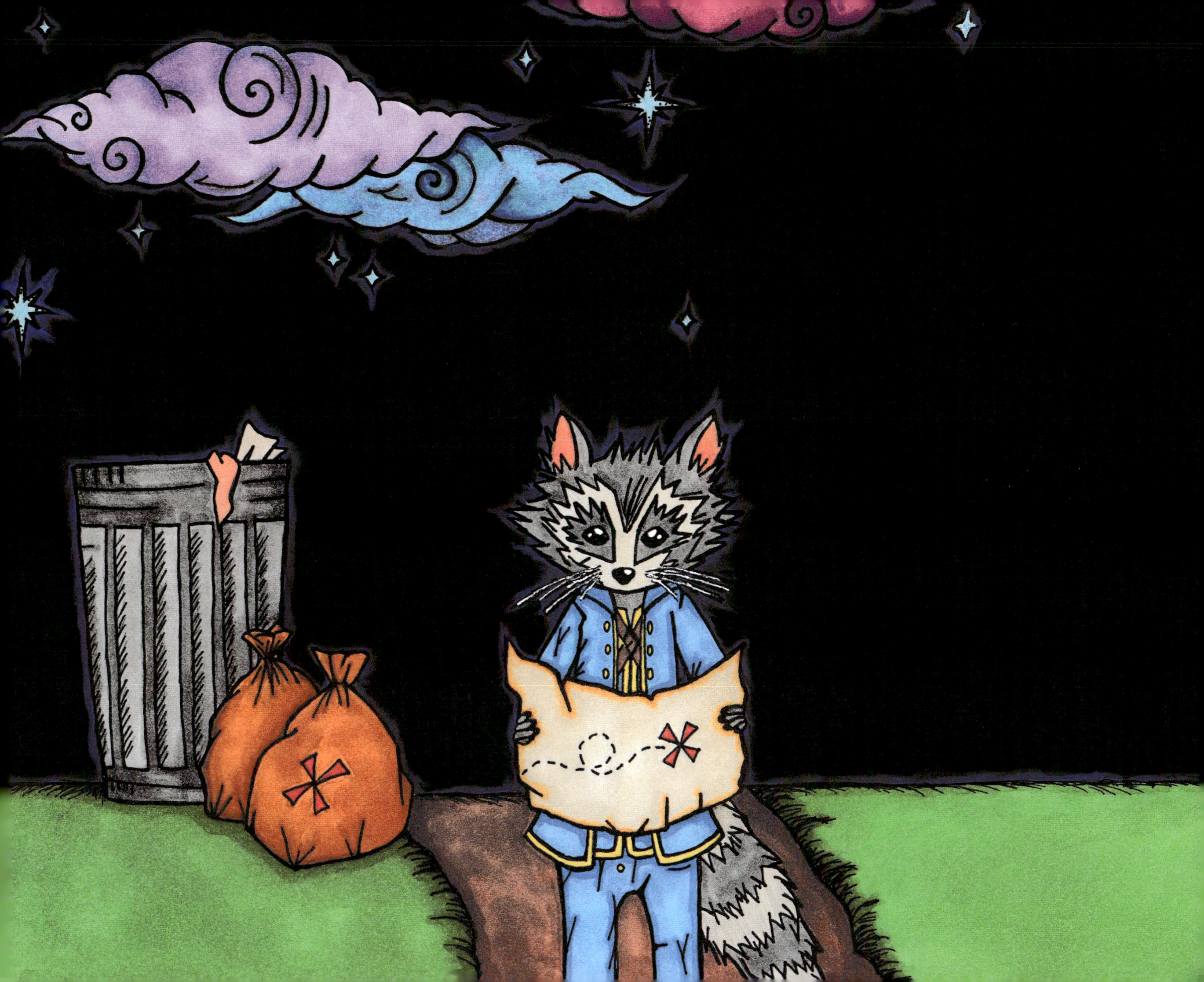

Not even cats are up for this job!

How can cats watch over the night when they are really too busy showing off their dance skills for you?

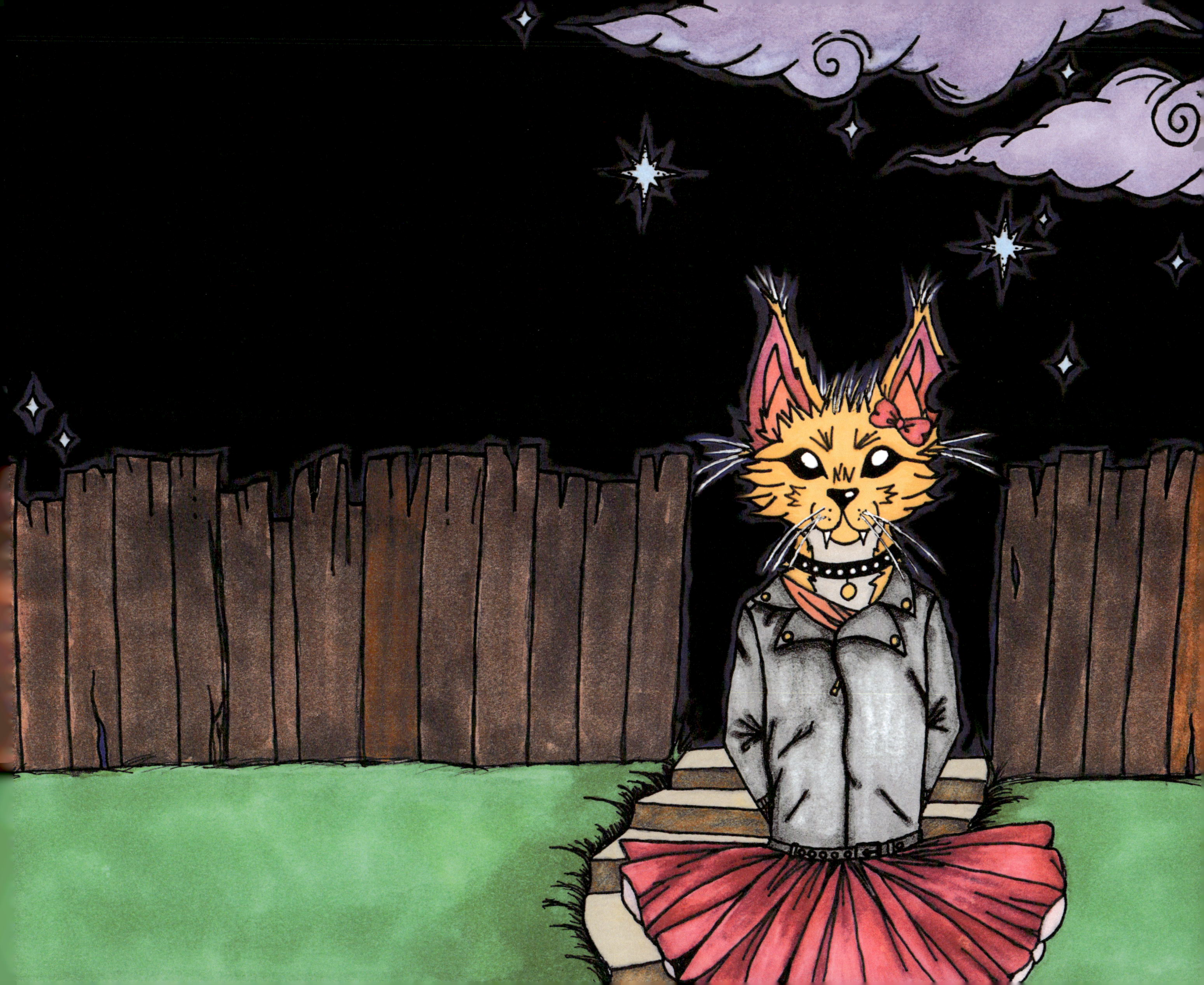

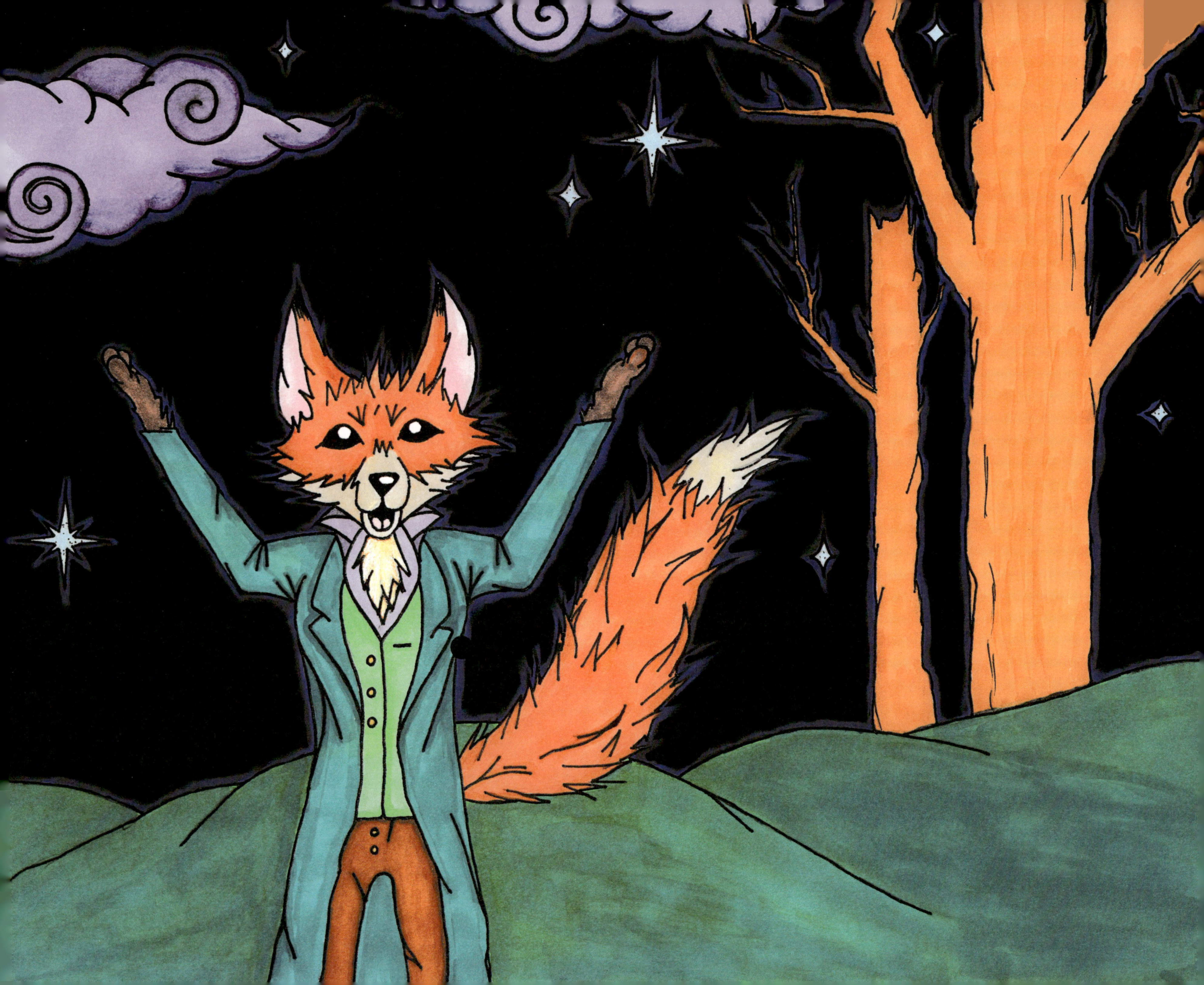

And don't get me started on foxes. Foxes would **NEVER** watch over the night!

Foxes are always thinking about the next joke they can play on someone! Don't ever take a fox seriously.

Trust me on this!

They think it is very funny to hide your glasses.

Then you can't find them because you don't have glasses to look for them.

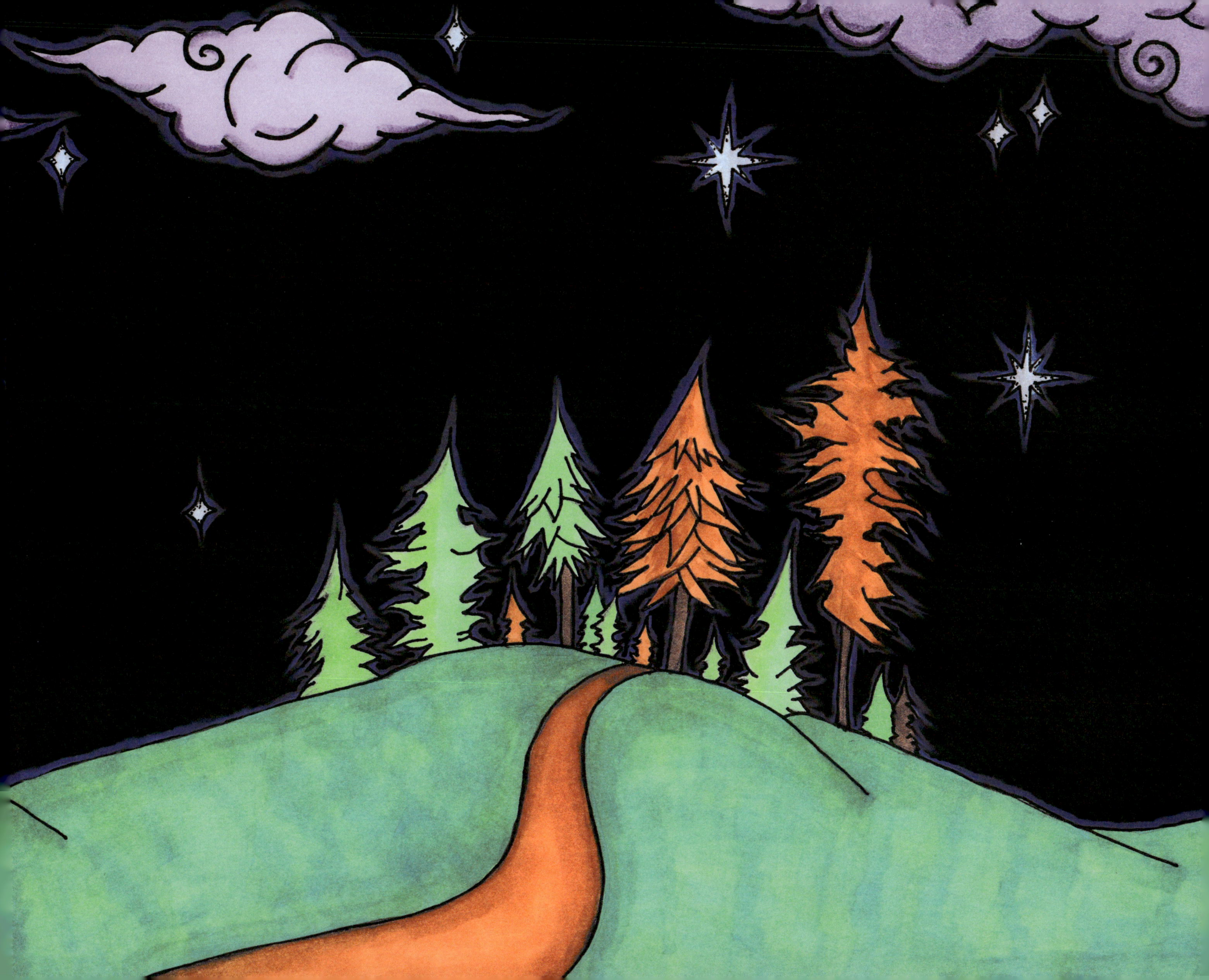

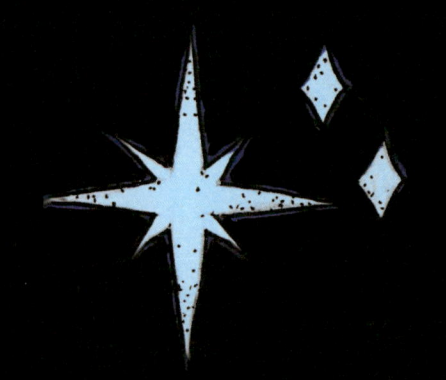

How do I know this?

Just a lucky guess.

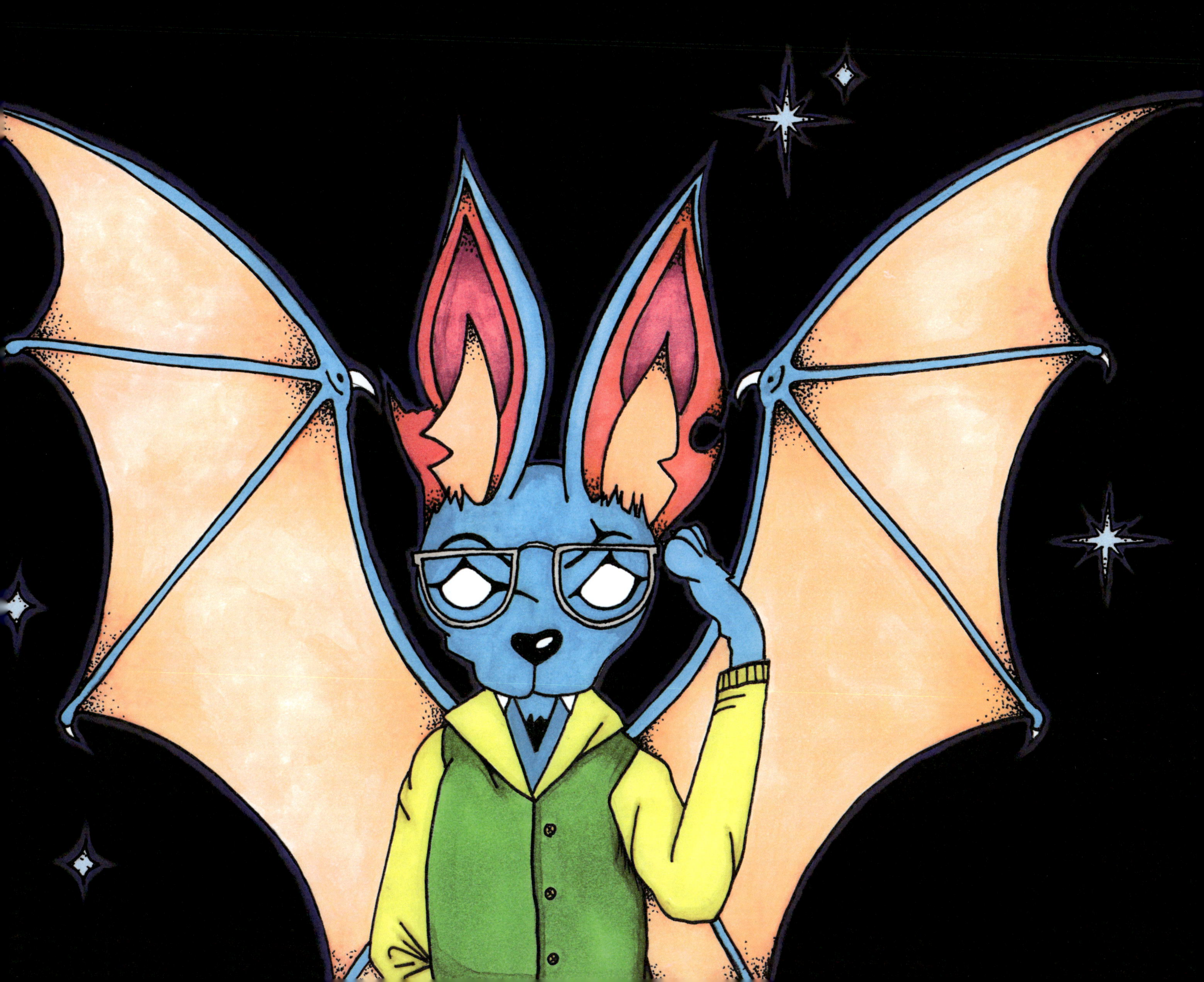

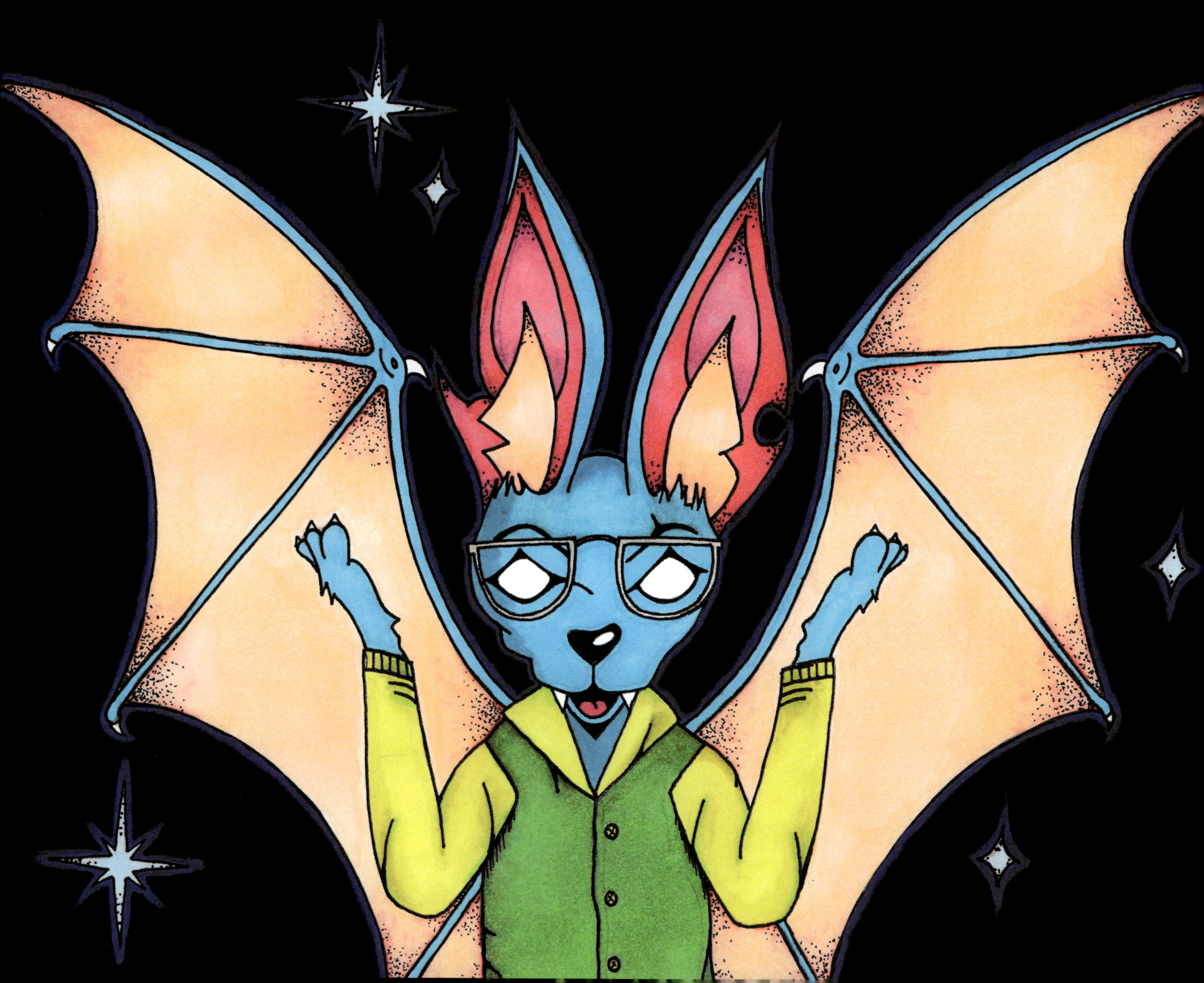

What do you think about bats now?

You think they are scary?!

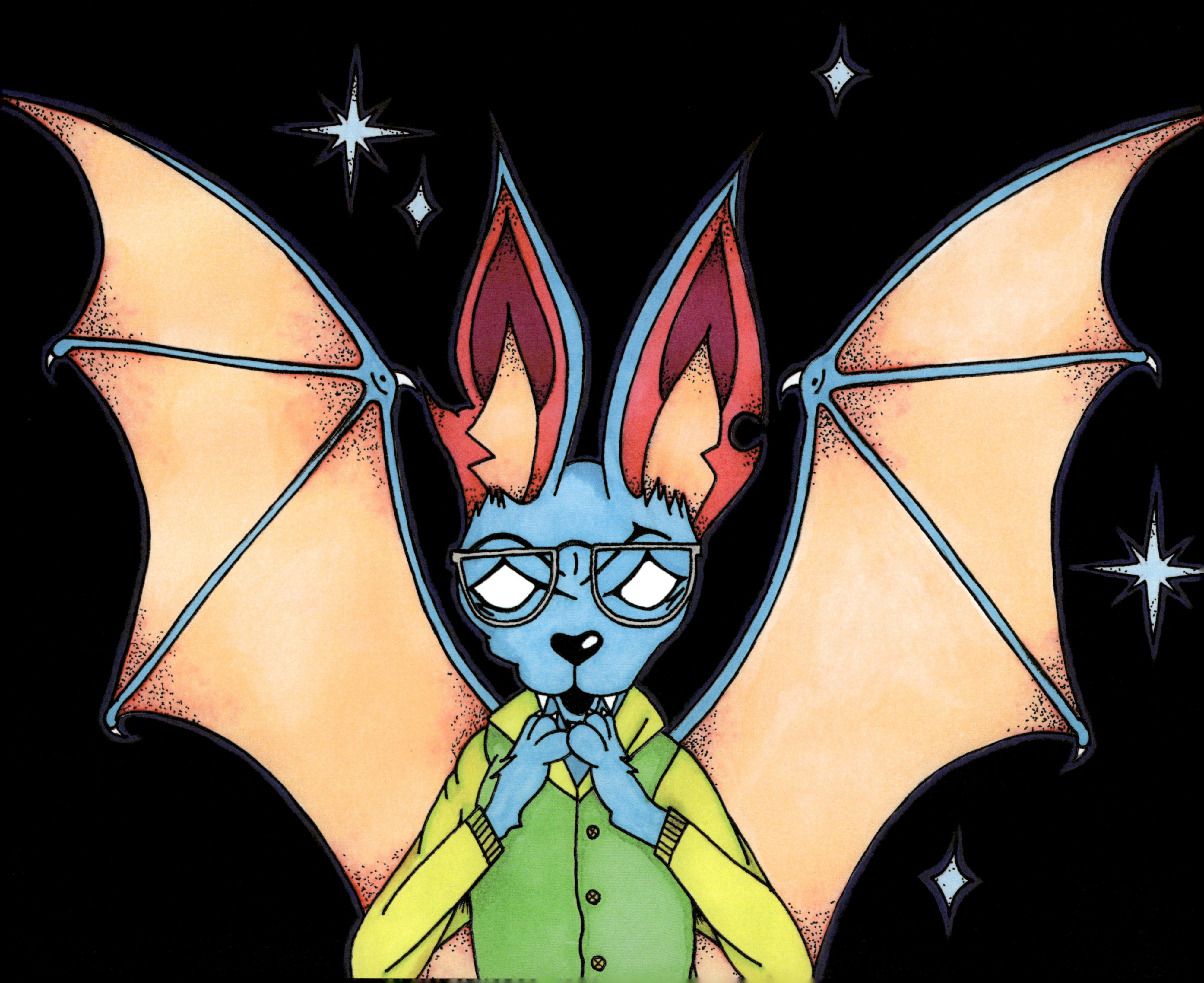

Well, they are not. Bats are SUPER COOL.

How could you think that bats are scary?

Maybe bats think that you are scary.

Why should you like bats?
Well, bats make sure you have some amazing dreams!

Remember that time you rode a dinosaur?
Yep, the bats helped that happen!

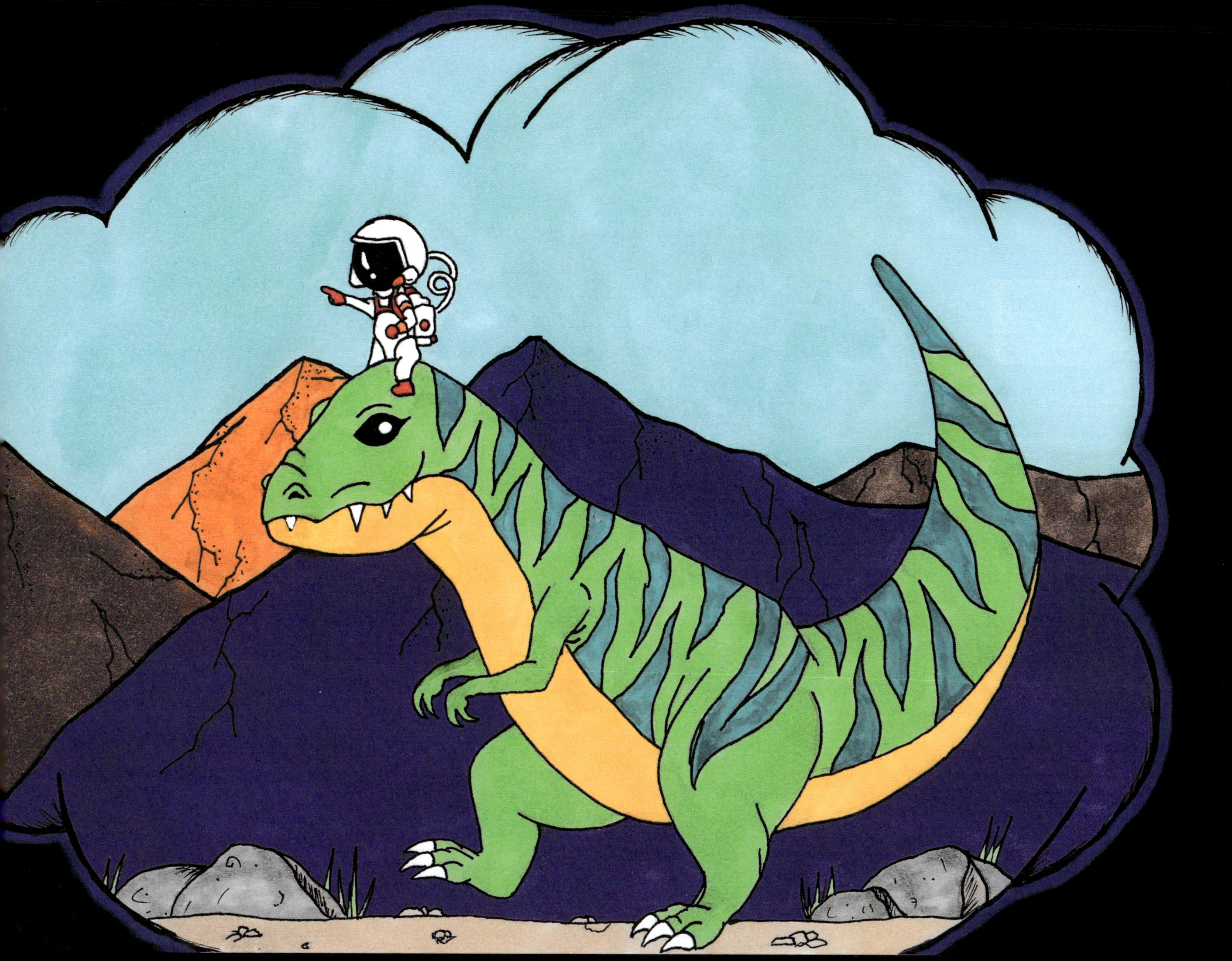

Bats also help those nighttime clouds look extra cool! They swirl around them to create the coolest designs!

Bats do all sorts of things to make you happy at night; you just didn't know it.

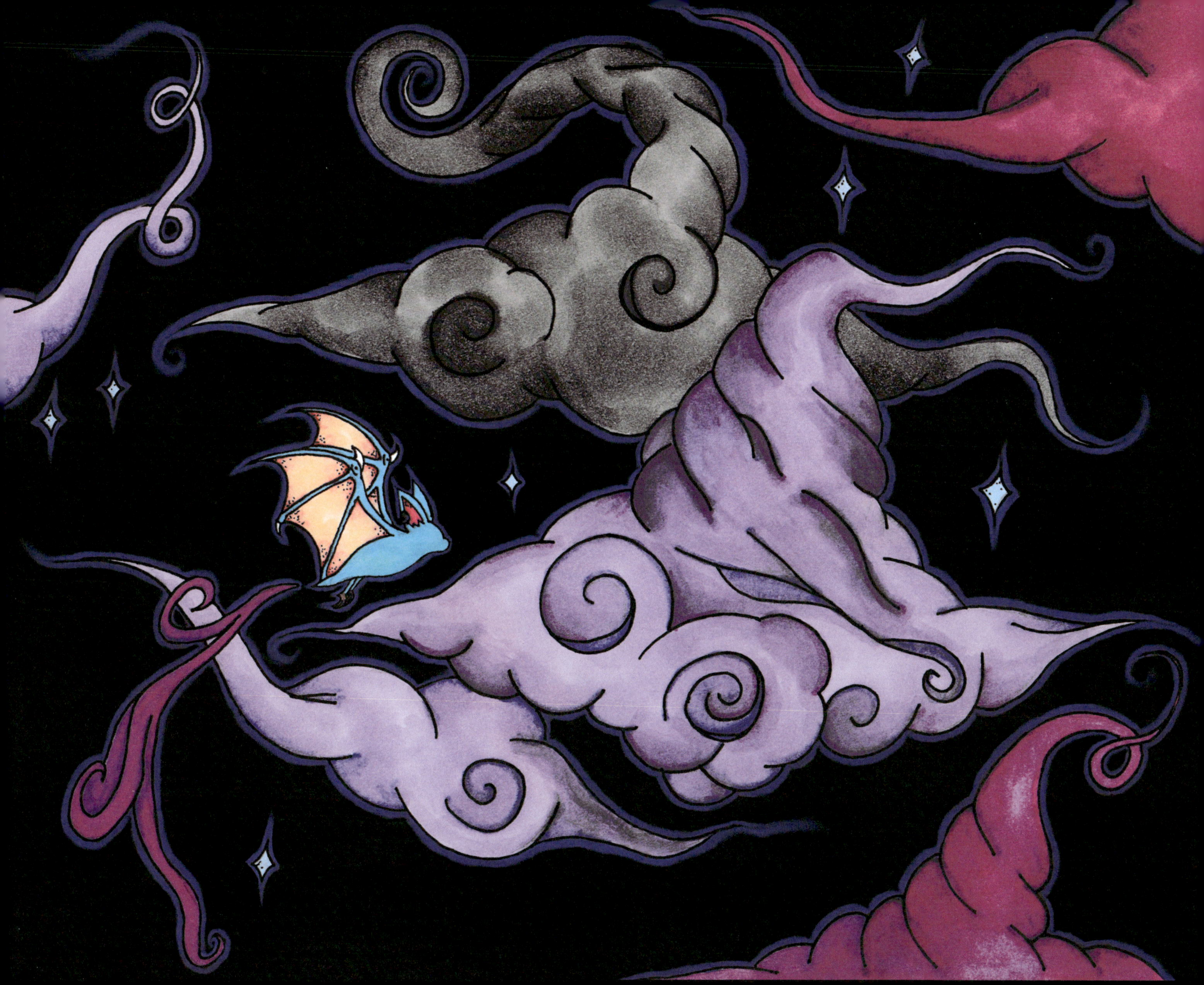

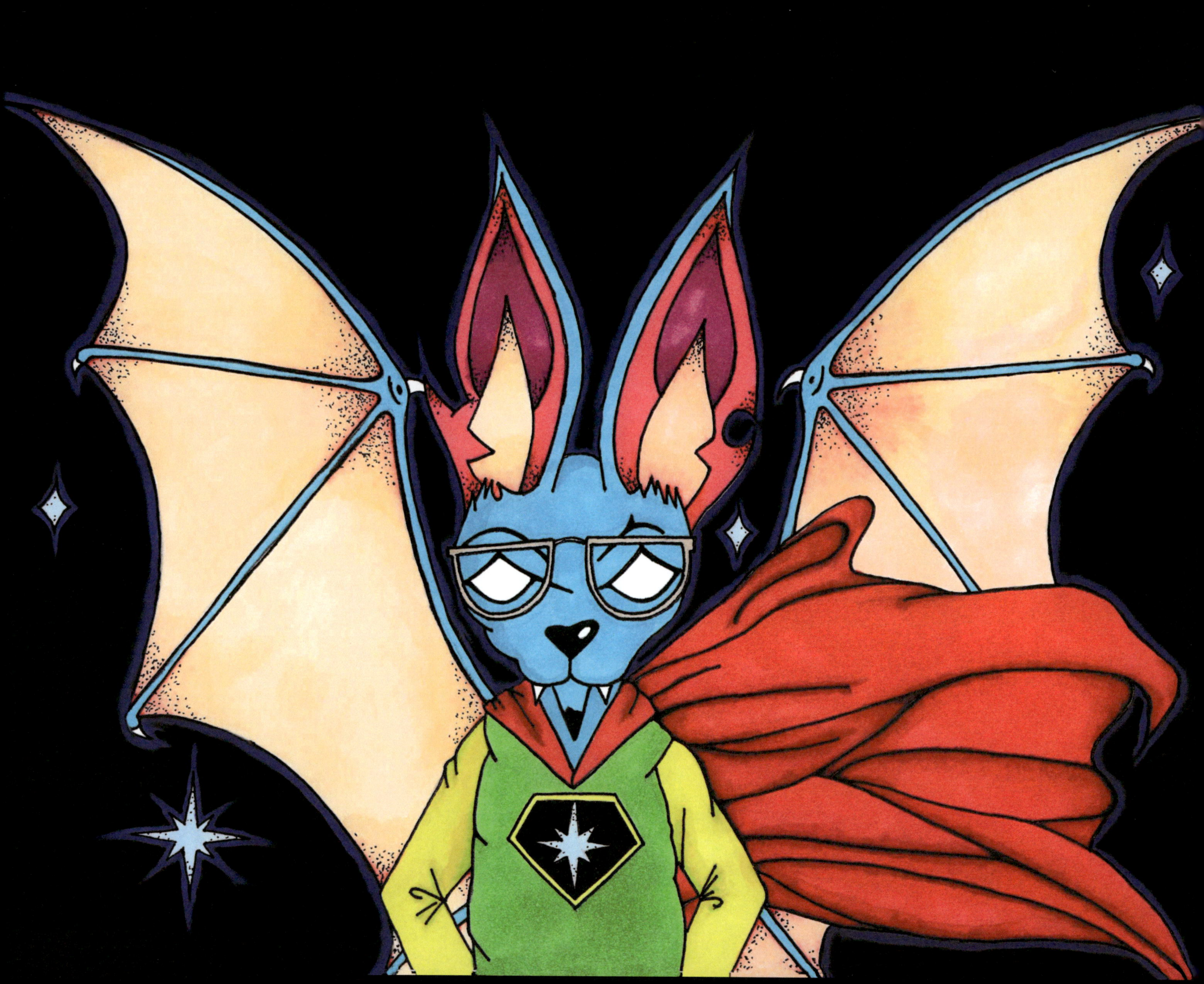

Bats also make sure that you are watched over at night. They do their best to make sure that those bad dreams stay away!

While each day is a new day, the bats try to make the night special too.

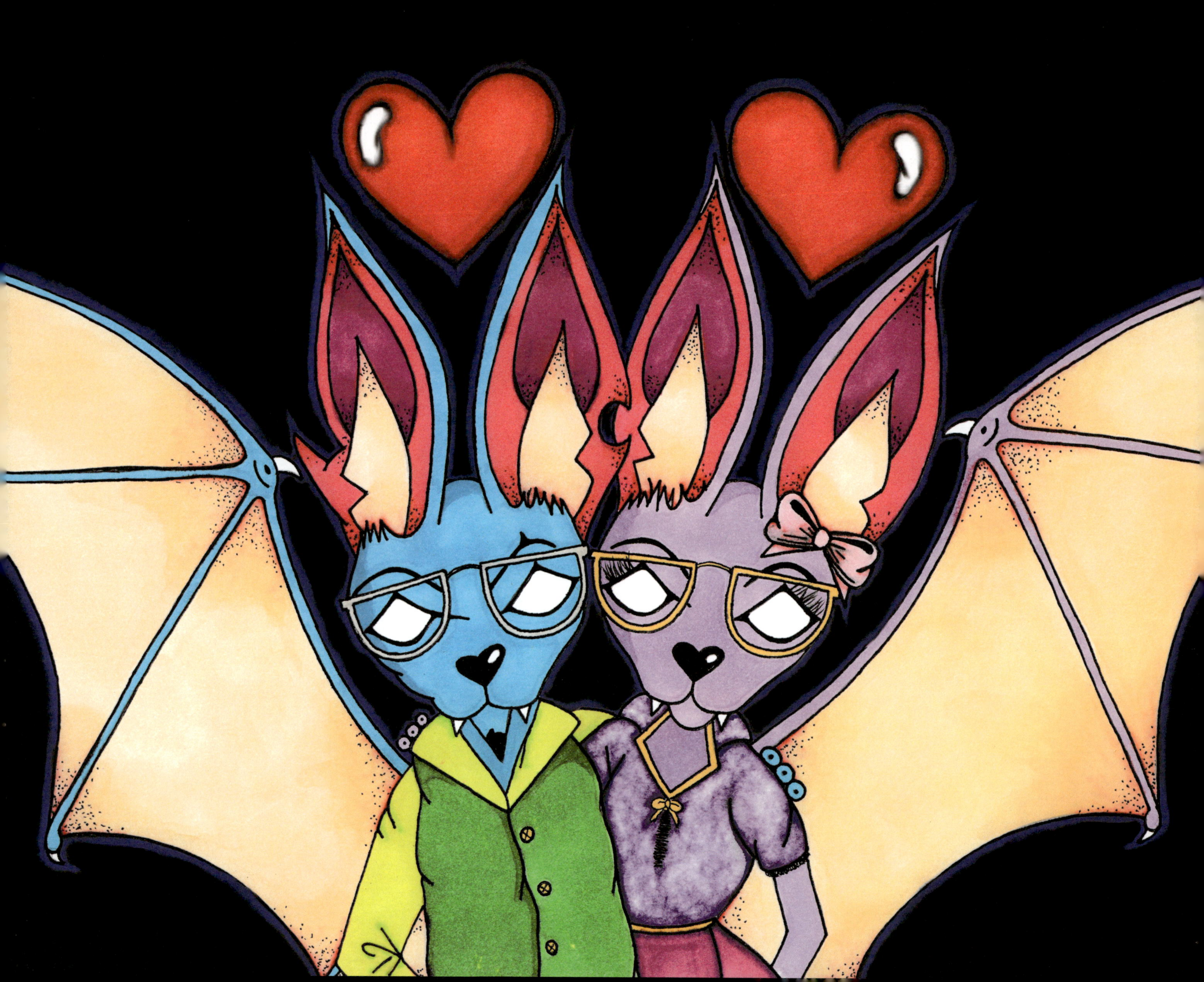

After all, when you have that beautiful moon lighting up the sky, the stars twinkling, and your friends, the bats, watching over you, the possibilities of your dreams are endless.

And when you are dreaming about your next adventure, we know you are pretty special too.

www.ingramcontent.com/pod-product-compliance
Ingram Content Group UK Ltd.
Pitfield, Milton Keynes, MK11 3LW, UK
UKRC030302190225
455207UK00001B/2